C000186105

STRATFORD
UPON AVON TO
CHELTENHAM

Vic Mitchell and Keith Smith

MP Middleton Press

*Cover picture: "Castle" class no. 5086 **Viscount Horne** stands at Cheltenham Spa Malvern Road at 12.8pm on 5th June 1949 with the 10.10am (Sundays only) Wolverhampton (Low Level) to Penzance restaurant car train. It called at Stratford-on-Avon at 11.30am and carried through coaches to Paignton. (R.S.Carpenter coll.)*

ACKNOWLEDGEMENTS

We are very grateful for the help given by many of those mentioned in the photographic credits and also for that received from G.Croughton, D.Jeynes, J.R.W.Kirkby, N.Langridge, D.Mee, Mr D. & Dr S.Salter, J.J.Smith, N.Sprinks, G.T.V.Stacey, E.Youldon and our ever supportive wives.

The authors and publishers regret that they are not able to supply copies of pictures contained in their publications, but requests for prints of photographs from the Mowat Collection can be made to W.R.Burton, 3 Fairway, Clifton, York and those marked Lens of Sutton can be obtained from 4 Westmead Road, Sutton, Surrey.

Published October 1998

ISBN 1 901706 25 7

© Middleton Press, 1998

Design Deborah Goodridge

Published by
        Middleton Press
        Easebourne Lane
        Midhurst, West Sussex
        GU29 9AZ
Tel: 01730 813169
Fax: 01730 812601

Printed & bound by Biddles Ltd,
        Guildford and Kings Lynn

CONTENTS

The 1946 map at 4 miles to 1 inch scale shows the route from top right to lower left.

GEOGRAPHICAL SETTING

Commencing at the old established market town of Stratford-on-Avon, the route soon crosses the west flowing River Avon and traverses the northern part of the Vale of Evesham, noted for its fruit and vegetable production.

The line becomes close to the Cotswold Hills after about ten miles and remains near their foot until the approach to the historic spa town of Cheltenham.

Much of the track was laid on clay, this giving rise to settlement and stability problems. The undulating route was devoid of severe gradients, this being achieved with only one significant tunnel near Winchcombe.

The maps are at 25ins to 1 mile, with north at the top unless otherwise indicated.

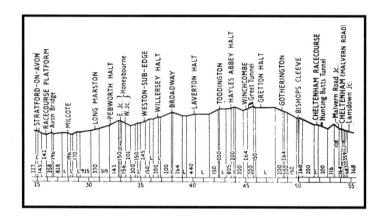

HISTORICAL BACKGROUND

The main line of the Birmingham & Gloucester Railway ran to the west of the route featured in this album and opened in 1840. Its Cheltenham station (later Lansdown Road) was not close to the town and in consequence a mile-long branch to St James Square was opened on 23rd October 1847. The Great Western Railway was involved with this line, together with the route to Gloucester, and in consequence there was an additional rail to accommodate its broad gauge trains. The BGR became part of the Midland Railway, which in turn became a constituent of the London Midland & Scottish Railway in 1923.

The Oxford, Worcester & Wolverhampton Railway was completed in 1852-53 and it opened a branch from Honeybourne to Stratford-on-Avon on 12th July 1859.

A branch from the Oxford to Birmingham route at Hatton was opened to Stratford-on-Avon by the independent Stratford Upon Avon Railway Company on 9th October 1860. The GWR operated the line, which was broad gauge until 1869, although most trains were standard gauge after 1863.

A connection between the two branches came into use on 24th July 1861. The SUAR became part of the GWR in 1883. The OWWR became the West Midland Railway in 1860 and part of the GWR in 1863.

The GWR obtained an Act on 1st August 1899 for the construction of a high speed line between Honeybourne and Cheltenham. The maximum gradient was to be 1 in 108 and the minimum radius of curves was set at half a mile. The route from Honeybourne was opened in stages: to Broadway on 1st August 1904, to Toddington on 1st December 1904, to Winchcombe on 1st February 1905, to Bishop's Cleeve on 1st June 1906 and to Cheltenham (Lansdown Junction) on 1st August 1906.

Combined with a new line north of Stratford to Tyseley in 1908, the GWR had developed a strategic route of some importance between the Midlands and the West of England. Doubling between Stratford and Honeybourne took place in 1907-08.

Local passenger services were a secondary consideration and were dieselised as early as 1934, most terminating at Honeybourne. Stopping trains were withdrawn south thereof on 7th March 1960 and northwards on 3rd January 1966. Most inter-regional freight trains were diverted to other routes after 8th November 1965 and parcels trains ceased on 6th March 1967. Some local goods traffic continued but long distance freights returned in May 1970.

The train service to both Cheltenham Spa Malvern Road and St James was withdrawn on 3rd January 1966, but a twice daily railcar ran between Gloucester and Leamington Spa until 25th March 1968. This could not thus call at Cheltenham. Through passenger services ceased altogether on 25th August 1975 and through freight traffic came to an end on 25th August 1976, following a derailment. Official closure south of Honeybourne was on 1st November 1976; the Long Marston - Stratford section was also closed at this time. A single line was retained between Honeybourne and Long Marston, mainly for the benefit of the Ministry of Defence.

Revival

The Gloucestershire Warwickshire Railway Society was formed on 18th August 1976 to prevent closure of, or alternatively, acquire the line. However, the track was lifted in 1979 but in 1981 the Gloucestershire Warwickshire Steam Railway PLC was incorporated to purchase the trackbed and buildings. The length between Broadway and the outskirts of Cheltenham was acquired on 24th February 1984 but the GWSR trades simply as the GWR. Their Light Railway Order was dated 24th December 1983.

Trains ran for a short distance south from Toddington from 22nd April 1984 and to the site of Hayles Abbey Halt from 1985.

Extension of services to Winchcombe took place on 2nd August 1987 and to a point south of Gretton in May 1990. Extension to a site near Far Stanley followed on 19th March 1994. Gotherington was reached on 12th July 1997.

The Stratford on Avon & Broadway Railway Society was formed in 1995 with the aim of ensuring the future of the route between those places. Sustrans (creators of the National Cycle Network) purchased the trackbed between Honeybourne and Broadway in 1998, with a view to accommodating both trains and cyclists on the route in due course.

PASSENGER SERVICES

Our journey is in the "down" direction and, unless otherwise stated, it is southbound trains running on most weekdays that are considered in these notes.

Stratford-Honeybourne stopping trains

While some trains ran only between these places, others originated at Leamington Spa or Birmingham and continued to Worcester or further. Sample frequencies are given below, the last figures being for the final Summer.

	Weekdays	Sundays
1859	5	1
1887	4	2
1907	8	1
1927	6	2
1947	9	0
1959	12	3
1965	15	0

Honeybourne - Cheltenham stopping trains

In the years 1904-06, as services were extended southwards, there were 9 or 10 trains, weekdays only. A connecting bus was provided between Winchcombe and Cheltenham, three times a day from 1st February 1905. Subsequent frequencies were thus -

	Weekdays	Sundays
1907	7	0
1927	8	1
1947	5	2
1959	6	0

A few trains started at Evesham and almost all terminated at Cheltenham St.James. From 1907 to about 1930, there was a through coach from London on one train per day, latterly slipped at Honeybourne.

Through trains

These commenced in 1908 with the introduction of a Wolverhampton - West of England train, which was to become a lasting feature of timetables. The service proved popular and was expanded to three or four trains each Saturday in the Summer for many years, the common destinations being Kingswear and Penzance. A Norwich - Cardiff train via Rugby and Leamington was tried in the Summers of 1908-09, but a lasting success was the Birmingham - Cardiff service, with some trains starting at Birkenhead prior to World War I. For most of this period, through trains were suspended.

As holiday traffic developed, so did the diversity of destinations; these included Ilfracombe, Minehead, Weston-super-Mare and Newquay.

The Wolverhampton-Penzance train was named "The Cornishman" from 30th June 1952.

The table below indicates the number of trains not stopping at intermediate stations, as shown in the Summer timetables.

	Weekdays	Sundays
1907	1	0
1927	7	0
1947	3	0
1959	4	2
1965	2	0

"The Cornishman" last ran via Stratford on 7th September 1962. Birmingham - Worcester services continued to run non-stop over the northern part of the route until 5th May 1969.

July 1927

HONEYBOURNE and CHELTENHAM SPA—(Motor Cars—One class only).

December 1947

HONEYBOURNE and CHELTENHAM SPA—(Third class only)

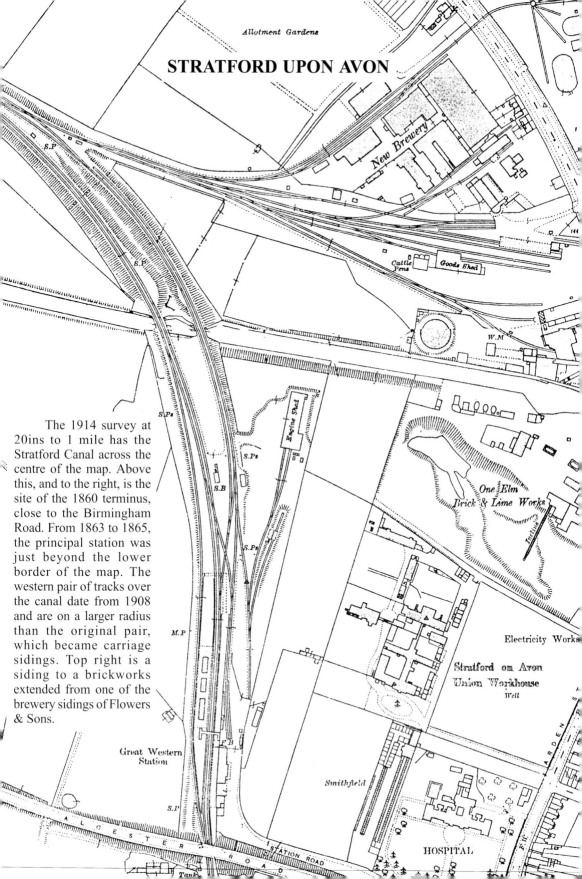

STRATFORD UPON AVON

Allotment Gardens

New Brewery

Cattle Pens

Goods Shed

W.M

Engine Shed

S.P

S.Ps

S.Ps

S.B

S.Ps

M.P

One Elm
Brick & Lime Works

Electricity Works

Stratford on Avon
Union Workhouse
Well

The 1914 survey at 20ins to 1 mile has the Stratford Canal across the centre of the map. Above this, and to the right, is the site of the 1860 terminus, close to the Birmingham Road. From 1863 to 1865, the principal station was just beyond the lower border of the map. The western pair of tracks over the canal date from 1908 and are on a larger radius than the original pair, which became carriage sidings. Top right is a siding to a brickworks extended from one of the brewery sidings of Flowers & Sons.

Great Western
Station

Smithfield

S.P

HOSPITAL

ALCESTER ROAD

STATION ROAD

Tank

1. The Birmingham Road station was used by all passengers from 9th October 1860 until 24th July 1861. Thereafter some trains ran to a station south of Alcester Road. The first terminus for GWR trains is seen left of centre in this 1934 view of the goods yard, which closed on 6th May 1968. (Mowat coll.)

2. A closer look at the original GWR terminus in 1934 reveals that it was used for goods traffic, mainly beer from the neighbouring brewery. It had continued to be used by a few excursion trains until 1869. (Mowat coll.)

3. A northward view from Alcester Road in 1934 includes the 1865 platform right, the 1891 one facing it and the 1908 one on the left. This had been a bay, with access from the north, until 1911. Crowds visiting the 1864 tercentenary celebrations of Shakespeare's birth had overwhelmed the tiny temporary station situated behind the camera. (Mowat coll.)

4. A roof spanned both tracks from 1865 to about 1900. Looking south in 1934, we see West Box beyond the 1861 Alcester Road bridge and fruit vans in the dock siding. The box was in use from 1891 to 18th May 1969. (Mowat coll.)

5. The engine shed was photographed on 6th April 1958, not long after the closure of the shed at Stratford's other station. This explains the presence of a 4F 0-6-0 and an ex-WD 2-8-0 from the London Midland Region. (R.C.Riley)

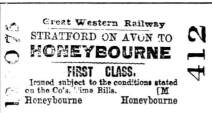

Great Western Railway
STRATFORD ON AVON TO
HONEYBOURNE
FIRST CLASS.
Issued subject to the conditions stated
on the Co's. Time Bills.   [M
Honeybourne   Honeybourne

412

6. Generous provision was made for the handling of luggage (and parcels) at this popular inland tourist town, where the river and theatre have drawn crowds for generations. However, the central poster recommends CAMPING COACHES elsewhere in the 1950s. (Lens of Sutton)

7. Wagons loaded with engine coal were pushed up the bank on the right and unloaded by a labourer onto a steel floor. It was then loaded into tubs on steel wheels and tipped into the locomotive tenders. The shed was in use from 1908 until 10th September 1962. (R.C.Riley)

8. The footbridge was erected in 1891, along with new buildings. The one on the right was part of the 1865 station. On the left is an emergency food store from World War II. The photograph dates from 1958. (R.C.Riley)

HONEYBOURNE and CHELTENHAM SPA—(Third class only)

Week Days only

Miles		a.m S	a.m E	E 5 30	S 5 30	9 15 am		p.m S	2 10 pm V	p.m 4 45		p.m 8 S			
	163 London (Pad.) .... dep														
	Honeybourne ...... dep	7 17	7 25	9 58	..	1040	..			5 35	7 20	8 15	..	..	
2¼	Weston-sub-Edge Halt..	7 22	7 30	10 4	..	1046	1 1	..	..	5 41	Bb	8 21	..	..	
4	Willersey Halt..........	7 25	7 33	10 7	..	1049	1 4	..	..	5 44		8 24	..	..	
5½	Broadway..............	7 30	7 40	1012	..	1053	1 9	2 15	..	5 48	7 29	8 28	1110	..	
7½	Laverton Halt.........	7 35	7 45	1017	..	1058	1 13	2 19	..	5 53		8 34	..	..	
10	Toddington...........	7 40	7 50	1022	..	11 3	1 18	2 25	..	5 58	7 37	8 39	1118	..	
11	Hayles Abbey Halt.....	7 43	7 53	1025	..	11 6	1 21	2 28	..	6 1		8 42	..	..	
12½	Winchcombe	7 47	7 57	1029	..	1110	1 25	2 32	..	6 5	7 43	8 47	1125	..	
13½	Gretton Halt..........	7 51	8 1	1033	..	1114	1 30	2 36	..	6 9	7 47	8 51	..	..	
16	Gotherington.........	7 56	8 6	1038	..	1119	1 35	2 40	..	6 14		8 56	..	..	
17½	Bishop's Cleeve.......	8 0	8 10	1042	..	1123	1 39	2 44	..	6 19	7 54	9 0	1135	..	
21¼	Cheltenham Spa E....	8 8	8 18	1050	..	1131	1 47	2 54	..	6 28	8 5	9 8	..	..	
21½	" Spa D arr	8 11	8 20	1053	..	1134	1 50	2 57	..	6 31	8 8	9 11	1145	..	

Week Days only

Miles		a.m	a.m	a.m	S	S	E	p.m	E	M	S	S	
	St. James' Cheltenham Spa.. dep		7 35	11 37	1 12	2 20	2 30	4 40	6 15	6 15	7 0	1020	
	" (Malvern Rd.)		7 38	11 39	1 15	2 22	2 35	4 45	6 18	..	7 2	..	
4½	Bishop's Cleeve.......		7 47	11 47	1 24	2 32	2 42	4 54	6 27	6 26	7 11	1032	
5½	Gotherington.........		7 52	11 52	1 29	2 37	2 47	4 59	6 32	6 34	7 16	1037	
	Gretton Halt..........		7 56	11 56	1 33	2 41	2 51	5 8	6 39	6 42	7 20	1041	
9½	Winchcombe	6 38	8 1	12 0	1 37	2 45	2 56	5 8	6 41	6 48	7 25	1045	
10	Hayles Abbey Halt.....		8 4	12 4	1 40	2 49	3 0	5 12	6 45	..	7 29	1050	
11½	Toddington...........	6 44	8 8	12 8	1 44	2 53	3 4	5 16	6 48	6 59	7 33	1054	
14½	Laverton Halt.........		8 13	12 13	1 49	2 58	3 9	5 20	6 53		7 38	11 0	
16	Broadway.............	6 55	8 20	12 18	1 53	3 3	3 16	5 27	7 12	7 15	7 45	11 4	
17½	Willersey Halt........	6 58	8 24	12 22	..	3 7	3 20	5 31	7 16		7 49	..	
19	Weston-sub-Edge Halt..	7 1	8 27	12 25	..	3 10	3 23	5 34	7 19		7 53	..	
21½	Honeybourne ...... arr	7 7	8 32	12 31	..	3 15	3 30	5 40	7 26		8 0	..	
123½	163 London (Pad.).. arr	10 0	1130	3 38	..	7 45	7 45	9 D5	1130				

A Arrives 6 57 p.m.   **B** Malvern Road   Bb Calls to set down only on notice being given by the passenger to the Guard at Honeybourne   **D** St. James'   ⁋ Refreshment Car to and from Moreton-in-Marsh   **E** Except Saturdays   **M** Saturdays only. By Bristol Tramways Omnibus.   Hand luggage only, conveyed   **R** Refreshment Car   **S** Saturdays only   V Via Leamington Spa (General)   V Refreshment Car to Leamington Spa (Gen.)

On Sundays the Bristol Tramways and Carriage Co. Ltd. operate a Road Service between Cheltenham Spa, Winchcombe and Broadway, also the Birmingham and Midland Motor Omnibus Co. Ltd. (Midland Red) operate a Road Service between Broadway and Evesham

June 1952. Note that the 6.15pm up local train was replaced by a bus on Saturdays, presumably because the line was too busy with holiday trains.

9. Two railcars stand at platform 3 on 28th May 1966, this platform being used for the Worcester trains at that time. The food store siding came into use on 20th July 1942 and can be seen top left. (J.M.Tolson/F.Hornby)

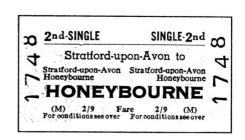

10. East Box was situated near the canal bridge and had replaced the previous East Box shown on the map, which had 35 levers, and also Goods Junction Box (29 levers) on 13th August 1933. Having previously been used at Acton West, it had 55 levers and was in use until 6th April 1998. (J.Moss/R.Carpenter coll.)

11. Showing a West Midland logo, no. W50852 waits to depart for Birmingham at 15.19 on 23rd September 1981. The platform buildings had been demolished and platform 3 had been designated 3a and 3b. It had reverted to being a bay on 18th May 1969. (T.Heavyside)

12. After the total ban on steam on BR was lifted, Stratford ws the destination of the first such special train on 30th August 1970. Many have appeared since; this is the Great Western Society's from Newton Abbot to Birmingham via Didcot, where no. 5051 *Earl Bathurst* took over the train on 9th October 1982. (D.Mitchell)

13. No. 150202 stands in deep shadow as it waits to leave for Stourbridge Junction at 09.24 on 7th July 1998. After an absence of many years, through trains from London via Hatton had by then been reintroduced, using Thames Turbo units. (V.Mitchell)

SOUTH OF STRATFORD UPON AVON

14. Passing under Alcester Road on 26th October 1974 is an LCGB railtour, which had arrived at Stratford behind "Merchant Navy" class no. 35028 *Clan Line*. No. D1025 took it south over a route then seldom traversed by passengers. The line had been doubled south to the next junction in 1899. (T.Heavyside)

15. After the track was lifted south of Stratford in 1980, two buffer stops were fitted. Later a point was provided to link the two lines and facilitate engine release. This 1998 view from Alcester Road includes the pre-1908 site of the engine shed - left. West Box had been on the right, with a refuge siding beyond it. (V.Mitchell)

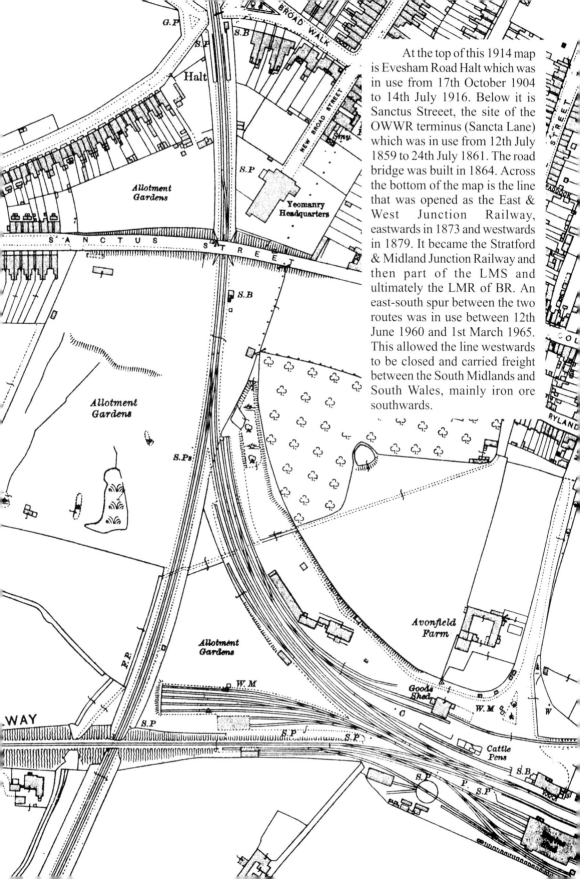

At the top of this 1914 map is Evesham Road Halt which was in use from 17th October 1904 to 14th July 1916. Below it is Sanctus Streeet, the site of the OWWR terminus (Sancta Lane) which was in use from 12th July 1859 to 24th July 1861. The road bridge was built in 1864. Across the bottom of the map is the line that was opened as the East & West Junction Railway, eastwards in 1873 and westwards in 1879. It became the Stratford & Midland Junction Railway and then part of the LMS and ultimately the LMR of BR. An east-south spur between the two routes was in use between 12th June 1960 and 1st March 1965. This allowed the line westwards to be closed and carried freight between the South Midlands and South Wales, mainly iron ore southwards.

16. Evesham Road Box position is marked S.B. at the top of the map. On the left is the 13-lever box of 1891 shortly before it was replaced by a new 50-lever one on 12th June 1960. This was designed to control the junctions to the south (pictures 17 and 21) and was in use until 22nd September 1976. The street lamp (right) has one red glass as warning to road users of the crossing. (British Rail)

17. The box nameplate states STRATFORD-UPON-AVON SM JCN in this April 1957 view. It had 18 levers and was in use until 12th June 1960. From that date until 1st March 1965, there was only a single line connection to the SM route. The former SMJR line crosses the background, the connections to it being behind the first coach. "Hall" class 4-6-0 no. 7918 *Rhose Wood Hall* is working an up train. Passenger services west to Broom ceased in 1949 and east to Blisworth in 1952. (R.C.Riley)

18. No. 9401 is accelerating a stopping train to Worcester on 14th December 1957 and is about to pass under the former Stratford & Midland Junction Railway line. The 9400 class was designed by Hawksworth and introduced in 1947, the last new design for the GWR. (R.C.Riley)

STRATFORD UPON AVON RACECOURSE

19. Although horse racing had taken place here since the 18th century, a station was not opened until 6th May 1933. This is the southward view in 1956; four years later Racecourse Junction was opened beyond the platforms. Further south, Chambers Crossing Halt was in use between 1906 and 1914. (R.M.Casserley)

20. Near the north end of the platforms was the bridge carrying the ex-SMJR single line, which closed completely on 13th June 1960. This may become the site of the northern terminus of the restored railway, as new roads occupy most of the route north. (R.M.Casserley)

21. The platforms are on the left as we witness a freight train running west, shortly before the completion of the new connection. The catch point was provided owing to the rising gradient beyond. (British Rail)

22. South of the station, the line crossed the River Avon and the River Stour. An inspection coach, with gauging attachments, was photographed in about 1908. This poor copy was first printed at that time. (C.Maggs coll.)

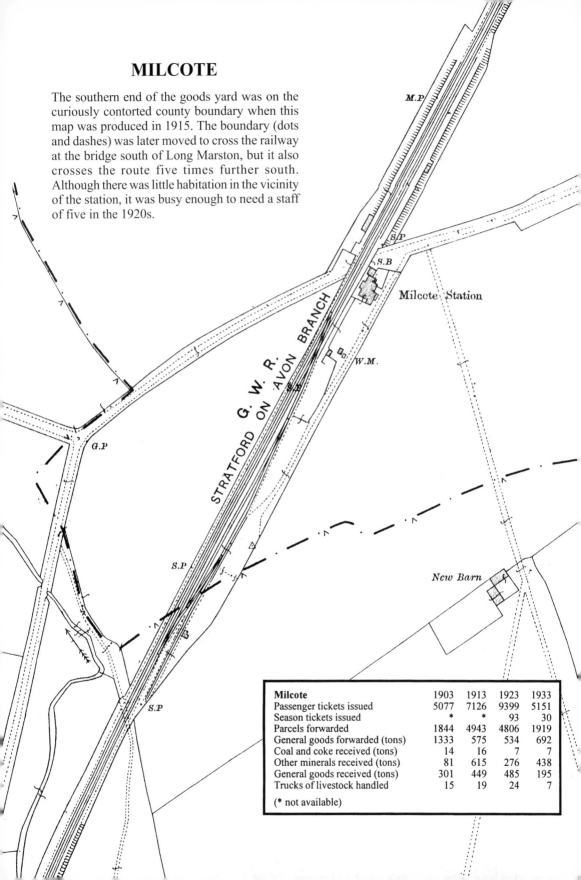

MILCOTE

The southern end of the goods yard was on the curiously contorted county boundary when this map was produced in 1915. The boundary (dots and dashes) was later moved to cross the railway at the bridge south of Long Marston, but it also crosses the route five times further south. Although there was little habitation in the vicinity of the station, it was busy enough to need a staff of five in the 1920s.

M.P

S.P

S.B

Milcote Station

G. W. R.

STRATFORD ON AVON BRANCH

W.M.

S.B

G.P

S.P

New Barn

S.P

Milcote	1903	1913	1923	1933
Passenger tickets issued	5077	7126	9399	5151
Season tickets issued	*	*	93	30
Parcels forwarded	1844	4943	4806	1919
General goods forwarded (tons)	1333	575	534	692
Coal and coke received (tons)	14	16	7	7
Other minerals received (tons)	81	615	276	438
General goods received (tons)	301	449	485	195
Trucks of livestock handled	15	19	24	7

(* not available)

23. We look north in about 1924 from the original platform, which was taken out of use in May 1908 when two new ones were opened beyond the level crossing. (Stations UK)

24. A 1934 view in the opposite direction includes the goods yard, which was closed on 1st July 1963. The main building, which was unstaffed from 1st March 1956, is on the left of the previous picture. The signal box had a gate wheel and 21 levers. It was erected in 1891 and reduced to a ground frame in 1973. It was manned until 1976 and, subsequently, the frame went to the Birmingham Railway Museum. (Mowat coll.)

25. Looking across the first platform in April 1968, we can enjoy the flamboyant style of the barge boards on the original building, which served as staff accommodation but was sadly soon to be destroyed. (C.Maggs)

26. The station was closed to passengers on 3rd January 1966 and some platform clearances were subsequently increased. The 1908 buildings were still intact when photographed after 60 years. (C.Maggs)

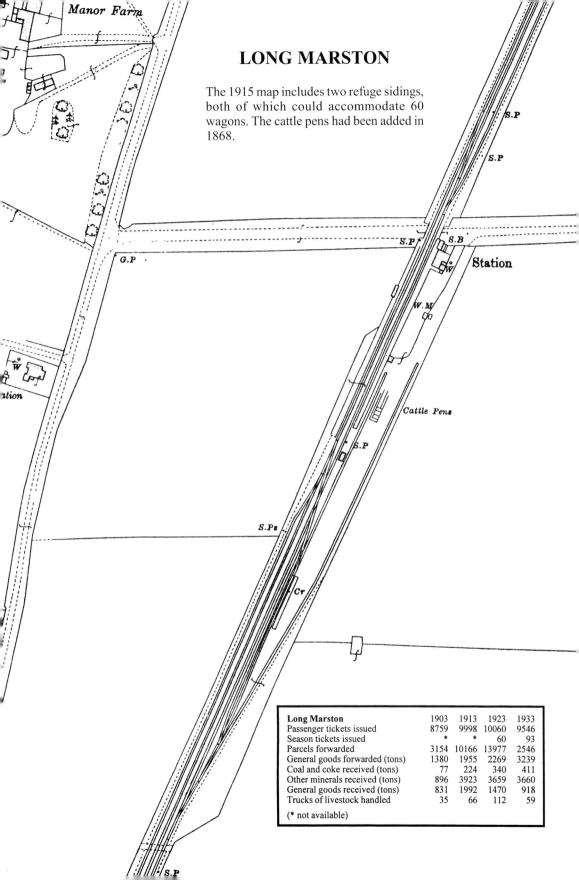

LONG MARSTON

The 1915 map includes two refuge sidings, both of which could accommodate 60 wagons. The cattle pens had been added in 1868.

Manor Farm

S.P

S.P

S.P

S.B

Station

G.P

W

W.M

W

Cattle Pens

S.P

S.Ps

Cr

ation

S.P

Long Marston	1903	1913	1923	1933
Passenger tickets issued	8759	9998	10060	9546
Season tickets issued	*	*	60	93
Parcels forwarded	3154	10166	13977	2546
General goods forwarded (tons)	1380	1955	2269	3239
Coal and coke received (tons)	77	224	340	411
Other minerals received (tons)	896	3923	3659	3660
General goods received (tons)	831	1992	1470	918
Trucks of livestock handled	35	66	112	59

(* not available)

27. Two platforms were provided from 1872 when a passing loop was installed, but the new one was south of the original one, right. A new up platform (left) was built in 1892 when the loop was lengthened. (Lens of Sutton)

28. The signal box was in use from 1892 until 16th November 1981; its frame was enlarged from 25 to 32 levers in 1936. It had ground frame status from March 1980 until closure on 16th November 1981. It was demolished in 1989. (Lens of Sutton)

29. "The Cornishman" speeds north and passes a train of empty stock waiting in the up refuge siding in about 1960. The crane had a capacity of 30cwt. (J.Moss/R.Carpenter coll.)

30. A more typical express of the 1960s was formed of DMUs; this one is running from Birmingham Snow Hill to Swansea High Street. The nearby goods yard was closed on 7th September 1964. The footbridge dates from the 1930s. (J.Moss/R.Carpenter coll.)

31. Apart from the addition of an exclusive toilet for the signalman, few changes were made before passenger trains ceased to call on 3rd January 1966. The trackbed from here to Stratford is now the Greenway cycle and foot path and rails were still to be seen in the level crossing in 1998, but the station site was occupied by a modern factory. (J.Moss/R.Carpenter coll.)

32. The Army established a massive 455 acre store depot east of the line in 1940 and an up goods loop (left) was formed from the former up refuge siding in 1941. To the right of class 9F 2-10-0 in the picture from about 1960 is West Ground Frame; East Ground Frame is between the end of the train and the station. (J.Moss/R.Carpenter coll.)

May 1949

WEEK DAYS

			a.m.		a.m.		a.m.		a.m.		a.m.		a.m.
WOLVERHAMPTON (L.L.)	dep.		6 5		7 10		7 44		9 0		9 12		10 35
BIRMINGHAM (Snow Hill)	„		7 0		7 45		8 30		9 40		9 50		11 10
Stratford-on-Avon	„	Saturdays only and runs 18th June to 17th September inclusive only. Through Train Birmingham to Paignton	7 38	Through Train Wolverhampton to Paignton	8 30	Through Train Birmingham to Weston-super-Mare and Taunton	9 8	Saturdays only. Through Restaurant Car Train Wolverhampton to Penzance	10 22	Saturdays only. Through Train Wolverhampton to Paignton Via Leamington	9N35	Except Saturdays. Through carriages Wolverhampton to Paignton and Restaurant Car to Penzance	11 46
Cheltenham Spa (Malvern Rd.)	„		8 15		9 6		9 45		11 2				12 25
Bristol (Temple Meads)	arr.						10 58						1 35
Weston-super-Mare	„						11 40						2 U6
Taunton	„				11 19		12 41						2 38
Minehead	„				1 5								4 12
Ilfracombe	„				2K40								6K48
Exeter (St. David's)	„				12 3								3 20
Teignmouth	„				12 33								3 48
Newton Abbot	„		11 35		12 45								3 59
Torquay	„		11 55		1 5						2 59		4 40
Paignton	„		12 5		1 14						3 25		5 0
Plymouth (North Road)	„								3 30		3 35		7 30
Newquay	„								6 5				6 45
Truro	„								5 20				7 30
Falmouth	„								6 30				7 50
St. Ives	„								6 50				7 40
Penzance	„								6 25				

WEEK DAYS—continued | SUNDAYS

			a.m.		a.m.		p.m.		p.m.		a.m.	
WOLVERHAMPTON (L.L.)	dep.		10 35		10 50		9 40		10 40		10 10	...
BIRMINGHAM (Snow Hill)	„		11 10		11 25		10 25		11 30		10 50	...
Stratford-on-Avon	„	Saturdays only. Through Train Wolverhampton to Paignton	11 46	Saturdays only. Through Carriages Wolverhampton to Minehead and Ilfracombe	12 4	Friday Nights/Saturday Mornings only. Through Carriages Wolverhampton to Newquay and Penzance	11 7	Friday Nights/Saturday Mornings only and will not run after 2nd/3rd September. Through Train Wolverhampton to Paignton	12 12	Through Restaurant Car Train Wolverhampton to Penzance. Through carriages to Torquay and Paignton	11 30	...
Cheltenham Spa (Malvern Rd.)	„		12 25		12 4		11 45		12 50		12 8	...
Bristol (Temple Meads)	arr.				1E50		12 57				1 20	...
Weston-super-Mare	„										2 0	...
Taunton	„				3 20		2D0		3 10		2 50	...
Minehead	„				4 45		7D28		7 28		4 45	...
Ilfracombe	„		6K48		6 16		8D26		8 26			...
Exeter (St. David's)	„		3 30				2D47		3 56		3 40	...
Teignmouth	„		4 2						4 10		4 10	...
Newton Abbot	„		4 14				3D20		4 30		4 20	...
Torquay	„		4 35				3D50		5 2		4 48	...
Paignton	„		4 45				4D0		5 11		4 55	...
Plymouth (North Road)	„						4 25				5 30	...
Newquay	„						7 25				8 5	...
Truro	„						6 15				7 30	...
Falmouth	„						7 20				8 15	...
St. Ives	„						8 5				9 15	...
Penzance	„						7 20				8 30	...

D—Applies on 10th, 17th and 24th September only; Through Carriages from Wolverhampton to Paignton on these dates only. **E**—Bristol (Stapleton Road) **K**—Via Exeter (St. David's) and Southern Region **N**—Change at Leamington Spa. **U**—Bristol (Temple Meads) depart 1.38 p.m.

33. A view from the same bridge in 1968 features the five exchange sidings and the military engine shed. The connection to the down main line had been to the right of the signal until 18th May 1964. (It is on the right of the previous picture). After closure of the through route in 1976, all trains to the depot ran via Honeybourne and had to stop on the level crossing in the distance before reversing. The access story is continued in caption 37. (C.Maggs)

34. A railtour from London (Waterloo) visited the depot on 16th October 1971 and Army 0-6-0ST no. 98 *Royal Engineer* ran between the station and the depot. It later retired to the Isle of Wight Steam Railway. No. 154 Railway Operating Company of the Royal Engineers worked the 25 miles of track during World War II and astonishing tonnages in excess of 400,000 were despatched in both 1943 and 1944. (S.C.Nash)

35. Transport within the depot was provided for personnel. This platform at North Gate, near the station, was photographed in 1979. There was another at Main Gate, near the eastern boundary of the site, on which opportunities for photography have been rare. The Falklands War resulted in heavy traffic again. (C.Maggs)

The 1989 track diagram includes both gates to the MOD secure area and one halt. The building on the left became the Stratford on Avon & Broadway Railway locomotive shed and the one on the right was occupied subsequently by the Yorkshire Engine Company. The Shed in the centre was to become the SBR carriage workshop.

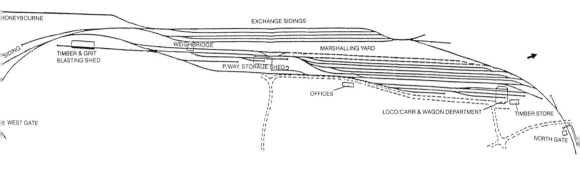

36. As part of the celebrations of the 200th anniversary of the formation of the Royal Engineers, ex-LMS class 8 no. 8233 hauled passengers to and from Honeybourne on 3rd and 4th October 1987. It is demonstrating its wartime role moving military equipment. The train is on the line shown lower right on the adjacent picture. This track served Bird's Scrapyard and many items of rolling stock made their last journey on it, but it became cheaper to move everything by road. (D. Trevor Rowe)

37. From the same view point as pictures 32 and 33, this panorama from 7th July 1998 reveals that the southern connection had been restored. This was completed on 20th November 1981, after which time the remaining down track to the station site and beyond was lifted. Stock of both the SBR and the Avon Valley Railway can be seen in the middle of the left page. In the background, beyond the rear coach, is the works of the Yorkshire Engine Company, successors to Thomas Hill Ltd., manufacturers and repairers

of diesel locomotives and rolling stock. Featured on the right page is the SBR motive power, Fowler no. 4 *Chorley* (left) and Barclay no. 201 *Mulberry*. The latter was one of a batch of four which were landed on a Normandy beach soon after D-Day, an achievement described in *Railways to Victory* (Middleton Press). In the background are coaches stored in the secure area, which had 22 miles of track. (V.Mitchell)

PEBWORTH HALT

38. Wooden steps led down to the road from the platforms, which were in use from 6th September 1937 until 3rd January 1966. Broad Marston Halt had been about 350 yds to the north and was open from 17th October 1904 to 14th July 1916, but it had very low platforms. (Lens of Sutton)

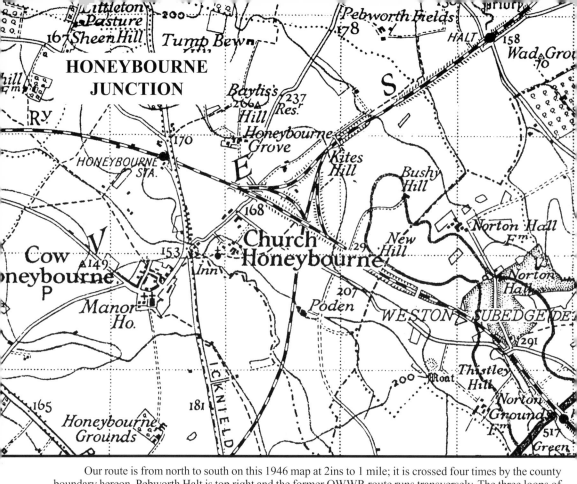

Our route is from north to south on this 1946 map at 2ins to 1 mile; it is crossed four times by the county boundary hereon. Pebworth Halt is top right and the former OWWR route runs transversely. The three loops of the junction were termed East Loop (top), West Loop (below it) and South Loop (right). There were four signal boxes: East Loop (top) and (from left to right) North Loop Junction, West Loop Junction and South Loop Junction. Only Station South Box was retained as a ground frame to give access to Long Marston and the spent ballast tip within the junction area, via West Loop Junction. To avoid reversals, East Loop was restored in 1981. The tip closed in March 1996.

39. Although not on the direct route, the station is illustrated as it was the terminal point for many local trains, indeed almost all of those from the south. This eastward view includes the 2.30pm from Cheltenham St.James on 27th February 1960, arrival being at 3.30pm. The station closed for goods on 1st January 1964 and to passengers on 5th May 1969, but the southernmost of the five platforms was reopened on 22nd May 1981. (E.Wilmshurst)

WESTON-SUB-EDGE

The 1923 edition includes two crossovers and a weighing machine (W.M.), together with one house and two cottages for some of the staff.

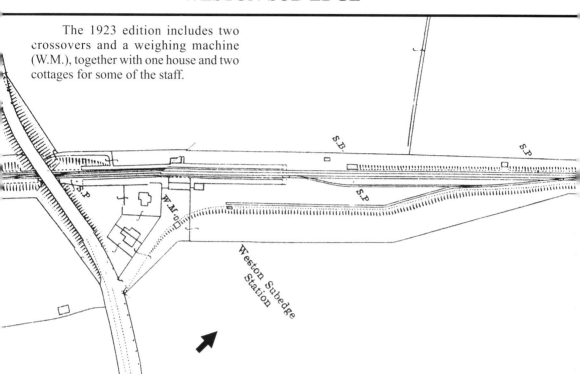

40. The prefix "Bretforton and" was applied until 1st May 1907. The necessarily high signboard was still to be seen when this northbound railmotor was photographed. The goods yard is on the right; it was served by a six-ton crane in its early years. The signal box had 27 levers and was in use until 8th October 1950. (Lens of Sutton)

41. Class 2800 2-8-0 no. 3860 runs south with empty coal wagons destined for South Wales on 18th July 1959. Local goods traffic had ceased on 25th September 1950, when the station also became unstaffed and was designated a halt. (H.C.Casserley)

42. A northward view from the B4035 bridge in 1963 includes the bridge carrying the Roman Icknield Street in the distance. There is no trace of this station from which an amazing 15366 tons of goods were despatched in 1941, presumably military stores. The up platform building was reused at Carrog on the Llangollen Railway. (R.M.Casserley)

Weston-sub-Edge	1913	1923	1933
Passenger tickets issued	4426	3035	1285
Season tickets issued	*	-	-
Parcels forwarded	5800	9091	2300
General goods forwarded (tons)	1276	645	331
Coal and coke received (tons)	48	65	-
Other minerals received (tons)	919	1255	1087
General goods received (tons)	490	685	167
Trucks of livestock handled	2	-	-

(* not available)

43. The bridge by the station is in the distance as we look south from Icknield Street. The locomotive is no. 90572, one of a large batch of "Austerity" 2-8-0s built during World War II for the Ministry of Supply. (J.Moss/R.S.Carpenter coll.)

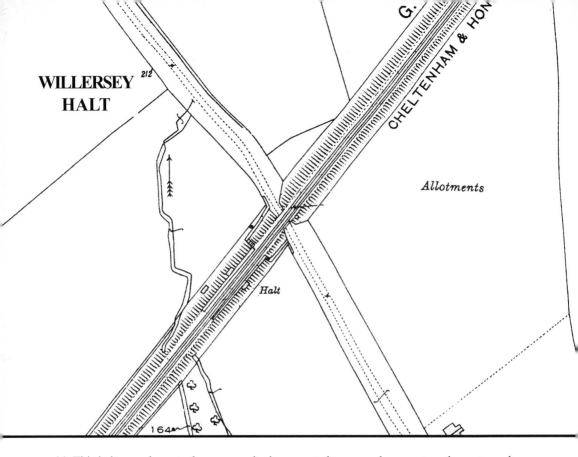

WILLERSEY
HALT *212*

Allotments

G.

CHELTENHAM & HON

Halt

164

44. This halt was closer to the community it purported to serve than most on the route and was open from 1904 to 1960. This is a northward view from 1959. (R.M.Casserley)

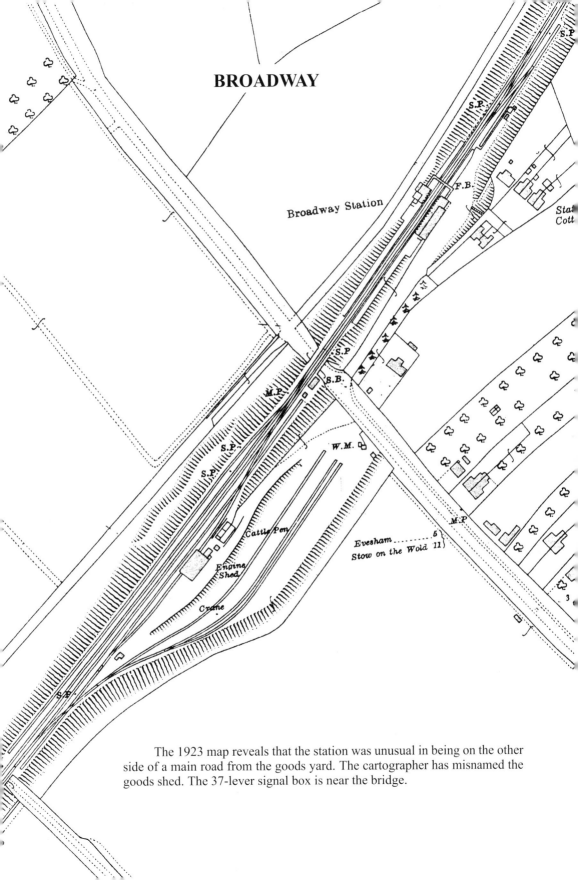

BROADWAY

Broadway Station

S.P

S.P

F.B.

Sta
Cott

S.P

S.P

B.B.

M.P.

S.P

W.M.

S.P.

Cattle Pen

Engine
Shed

Evesham........5
Stow on the Wold 11

M.P

Crane

3

S.P

The 1923 map reveals that the station was unusual in being on the other side of a main road from the goods yard. The cartographer has misnamed the goods shed. The 37-lever signal box is near the bridge.

45. During the short period that the station was a terminus, there were ten trains each weekday. This northward view is from a point close to the main road, which was numbered A44 from 1919 to 1998. A bypass, north of the town, opened that year; it included a bridge over the trackbed. (Lens of Sutton)

46. A view in the same direction, about 50 years after opening, shows more clearly the points of the short siding to the dock. Behind us is the goods yard, which closed on 1st June 1964, more than four years after passengers were able to board here. Much visited for its beauty, the town of under 3000 souls was nearly one mile distant. (R. Carpenter coll.)

47. The spacious station had a staff of 9 or 10 between the wars, when fruit and vegetable traffic was heavy. A wholesale market had been established close to the station. There was time to chat when this picture of an autotrain to Honeybourne was taken in the 1950s. The goods shed (behind the camera) survived to become the property of the GWSR. (Lens of Sutton)

Broadway	1913	1923	1933
Passenger tickets issued	17440	13686	7308
Season tickets issued	*	118	32
Parcels forwarded	17075	22605	13072
General goods forwarded (tons)	1139	970	305
Coal and coke received (tons)	198	704	804
Other minerals received (tons)	4917	3403	2188
General goods received (tons)	3599	2333	2465
Trucks of livestock handled	115	47	31

(* not available)

LAVERTON HALT

48. The halt was half a mile from the village and separated from it by a road numbered A46 until recently. Services commenced on 14th August 1905 and lasted until 7th March 1960. The paths would be busy on school days, as many local pupils travelled to Cheltenham for their education. (H.C.Casserley)

49. The 2.15pm local train from Broadway to Cheltenham was recorded on 18th July 1959. It ran on Saturdays only and had set out from St.James at 1.12; many children attended school on Saturday mornings at that time. (R.M.Casserley)

NORTH OF TODDINGTON

50. Stanway Viaduct was started in March 1903 and, on 13th November following, no. 10 arch collapsed without warning, soon after its formwork had been removed. The crane driver survived the fall and was sheltering under no. 9 when it also fell; rescued again, he was hit by no. 8 forty minutes later and died that night. There were three other fatalities.
(C.Maggs coll.)

51. No single cause was established for the accident but the formwork was left in place longer subsequently. This temporary track was laid on the east side and used for the conveyance of materials. No. 7 arch also fell and no. 6 cracked badly. All nearby were fitted with supports, if they did not already still have them.
(C.Maggs coll.)

52. The highest one of the 15 arches is 42ft and each are of 36ft span, giving a total length of 210yds. The structure crosses two small streams and was photographed in 1968.
(C.Maggs)

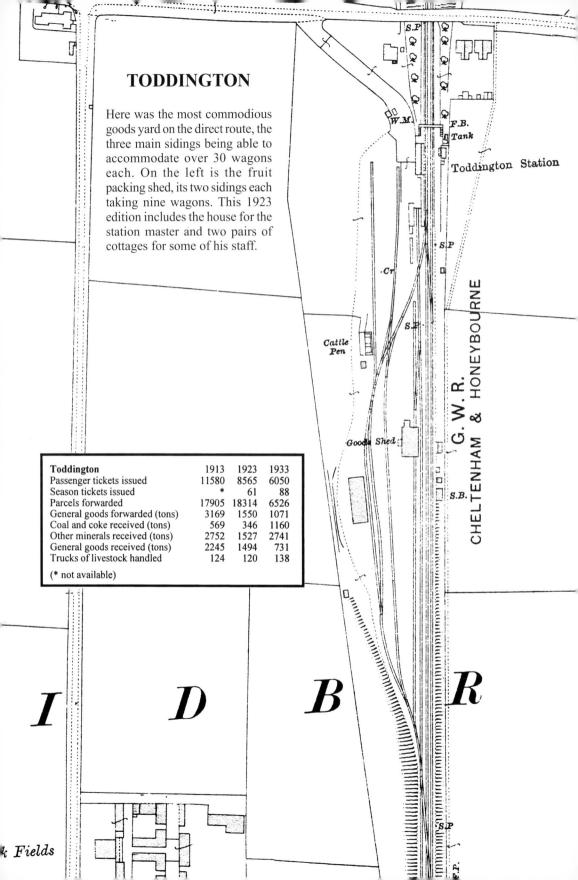

TODDINGTON

Here was the most commodious goods yard on the direct route, the three main sidings being able to accommodate over 30 wagons each. On the left is the fruit packing shed, its two sidings each taking nine wagons. This 1923 edition includes the house for the station master and two pairs of cottages for some of his staff.

Toddington	1913	1923	1933
Passenger tickets issued	11580	8565	6050
Season tickets issued	*	61	88
Parcels forwarded	17905	18314	6526
General goods forwarded (tons)	3169	1550	1071
Coal and coke received (tons)	569	346	1160
Other minerals received (tons)	2752	1527	2741
General goods received (tons)	2245	1494	731
Trucks of livestock handled	124	120	138

(* not available)

W.M.

F.B.
Tank

Toddington Station

S.P

·Cr·

S.P

Cattle Pen

Good Shed

S.B.

G. W. R.

CHELTENHAM & HONEYBOURNE

I *D* *B* *R*

S.P

k Fields

53. This southward view predates the footbridge, which was erected in 1912. The packing shed was occupied by different firms over the years and its roof can be seen beyond the main building. A six-ton crane was provided in the yard. (R.M.Casserley coll.)

54. Acetylene gas was generated for station lighting in the building to the left of the signal until 1917, when calcium carbide was difficult to obtain. This photograph is from June 1930. (C.Gilbert/R.S.Carpenter coll.)

55. A lengthy down freight rattles under the B4077 sometime in the 1950s. No. 5368 was one of the 4300 class 2-6-0s introduced in 1911 for this type of work. This locomotive was withdrawn in September 1958. (J.Moss/R.S.Carpenter coll.)

56. A photograph from 1958 includes a Hillman Minx from the 1930s and the 15-ton weighbridge. It also shows evidence of both oil and electric lighting and includes the former gas house. The goods yard remained in use until 2nd January 1967, after which time the weigh house and fruit packing shed were demolished. (H.C.Casserley)

57. To the left of the railings was a dock from which large quantities of milk was despatched. There was a staff of 10 throughout World War II, this increasing to 14 by 1952 but dropping to 5 when this picture was taken in 1958. (H.C.Casserley)

58. The yard was largely cleared of wagons on Cheltenham race days, in order to berth coaches. They were serviced while the locomotives went to Honeybourne for turning. Fruit traffic from the shed in the background was greatly reduced after the 1954 strike by railwaymen. This is the 1.02pm from Honeybourne on 18th July 1959. (H.C.Casserley)

59. An April 1968 picture reveals that the platforms had been cut away. This would facilitate the passage of out-of-gauge loads which commonly used this route. One siding was retained for the engineers and the signal box was worked until line closure on 22nd October 1976. The track was lifted in 1979-80. (C.Maggs)

60. A daunting task faced the GWSR in its fight to restore the line. This is the scene in 1982, when there were four ex-GWR locomotives on the site, together with many other items of rolling stock. A lease of the station area had been secured on 24th March 1981, but the 29-lever frame had gone to the Gwili Railway a few days previously. (C.Maggs)

61. Steam hauled trips were first operated on 22nd April 1984 after enormous efforts were made to relay track and tidy the site. This is the scene on 16th February 1985, as no. 5952 *Cogan Hall* awaits restoration having been decaying at Barry Scrapyard for many years. (T.Heavyside)

62. Although "Steam" was in the company's name, some recognised the need to preserve diesels, as many of the first generation were nearing the end of their lives. Nos. D9553, D9539 and 08114 were recorded in February 1985. The two class 14s were both still on the line in 1998 and in running order. (T.Heavyside)

63. The amazing achievements of the determined enthusiasts are evident in this photograph from 6th September 1987 featuring Peckett 0-4-0ST no. 1976 returning from Winchcombe, only a month after restoration of services thereto. (T.Heavyside)

64. Visiting locomotives are a regular feature of the GWSR programme of attractions. No. 7752 of 1930 was on loan from the Birmingham Railway Museum at Tyseley in 1991 and was photographed on 31st March. The water tank had previously served at Ashford. (T.Heavyside)

65. No. 47105 arrives with the 13.39 from Gotherington on 20th July 1997, a week after extension of working to that location. No. 45596 *Bahamas* is ready to depart from the down platform. (M.J.Stretton)

(Lower left)
66. Stepping onto the crossing on the same day, we can enjoy this fine view of *Bahamas* and its beautifully restored coaches; a splendid tribute to those who have laboured long and hard. The crossing has been superseded by a footbridge. (M.J.Stretton)

67. Viewed from the road bridge on 14th August 1997 is the north end of the operating line and no. 6960 *Raveningham Hall* running round its train. The berthed coaches stretch out towards Stanway Viaduct. (P.G.Barnes)

NORTH GLOUCESTERSHIRE RAILWAY

68. The Dowty Railway Preservation Society was formed in 1962 and restored both standard and narrow gauge stock on a site at Ashchurch, which had to be vacated in 1982. Members resolved to form the NGR, move to Toddington and concentrate on two-foot gauge. Their Jung-built 0-4-0WT *Justine* is seen on former Southend Pier rail on 6th September 1987. (T.Heavyside)

69. The railway has run along the western boundary of the station site for about 400 yds since October 1990, the lineside equipment coming mostly from local sources. Built by Henschel in 1918, this 0-8-0T was ex Feldbahn no. 1091 and was photographed in October 1995. The box had been on the Gloucester Eastgate line. (D.Trevor Rowe)

STRATFORD-UPON-AVON, HONEYBOURNE and CHELTENHAM SPA

Miles from Strat.-upon-Avon	Week Days	am	am		am	am RB	am		am		am		am RC		am		am		pm		am		pm		pm	pm RB
	152London (Paddington) .. dep										5 30				9 10						11 10				1 10	
	179Leamington Spa General.. dep		7A10			8N 7					9 20				11N20						1N 5				3N10	
	179Warwick .. .. „		7N14			8N11					9 24				11N24						1N 9				3N14	
	179Hatton .... „		7N21			8N17					9 34				11N33						1N16				3N20	
	179Wolverhampton (L.L.) .. „		5 40			7 25							9 0		10 10		11 36				11 36					2 35
—	179Birmingham (Snow Hill) „		6P20			8 10	②						9 40		10 53		12 25				12C25				2B45	3 45
—	Stratford-upon-Avon .. dep		7A45			8 46	8 52				10 6		1019		12 5		1 2		Saturdays only		1 47				4N 0	4 20
3	Milcote Halt		7N50				8 57				10 6				12 10						1 54				4N 6	
5½	Long Marston ..		7N56		3N27		9 3				10 12				12 16						2 1				4N12	
7	Pebworth Halt				3N31		9 6				10 16				12 20						2 5				4N16	
9	Honeybourne .. .. .. arr				8N35		9 10				10 20				12 25						2 9		Saturdays only		4A20	
14¼	163Evesham .... arr				8 55						10 32				12 36						2 25				4N33	
27¼	163Worcester (Shrub Hill) .. „	②			9 29				②		12 0				1 15				②		2 57				5N 5	
—	Honeybourne .... dep	7 25							9 45										1 17							
10¼	Weston-sub-Edge Halt ..	7 30							9 51										1 22							
11¼	Willersey Halt	7 33							9 54										1 25				②			
13	Broadway ..	7 40							9 59										1 29				2 45			
15	Laverton Halt	7 45							10 4										1 34				2 50			
17½	Toddington	7 50							10 9				THE CORNISHMAN						1 39				2 55			
18¼	Hayles Abbey Halt	7 53							1012										1 42				2 59			
20	Winchcombe	7 57							1017										1 46				3 5			
21¼	Gretton Halt..........	8 1							1021										1 50				3 10			
24¾	Bishop's Cleeve Halt	8 5							1028										1 56				3 18			
29	Cheltenham Spa { Malvern Road arr	8 16				9 19			1036				1058				1 35		2 4				3 26			4 53
29½	Cheltenham Spa { St. James' .. „	8 22							1042										2 10				3 32			

Week Days—continued	pm	pm RB	pm	pm	pm	pm	pm		pm	pm	pm		pm RB	pm		pm RB	pm	pm	Sundays am RB		pm	pm RB	pm		pm	
152London (Paddington) .. dep			2S45			3 10	4 45		4 10					6 23		8 10					2 10		6 10			
179Leamington Spa General.. dep	4 20					5N45			6N30				8 15	8 45		1019			8 45		5N 0	5b15	8N50		9 20	
179Warwick .. .. „	4 24					5N49			6N34				8 19	8 49				Saturdays only	8 49		5N 4	5b19	8N55		9 24	
179Hatton .... „	4 33					5N56			6N40					8 57					8 56		5N13	5b26	9N 3		9 31	
179Wolverhampton (L.L.) .. „	3A10	4 35	Via Oxford (Table 163)			5 10	Via Oxford (Table 163)		5 40				7 29						7 45		3 33	4 45	7 30		8 45	
179Birmingham (Snow Hill) „	4 8	5 5		5B 5	5B 5	5 45			6 25	6B40			8 30			9B10			9 0		4 5	6 5	8 5		10 5	
Stratford-upon-Avon .. dep	5 5	5 41		5 56	6 8	6 39			7 15	7N48			9 6	9H50		1045			9 36		5N35	6 42	9N23		11N10	
Milcote Halt	5 11			6 0	6 13	6 45			7 20	7N54				9H55				②			5N40		9N28			
Long Marston ..	5 17			6 5	6 18	6 52			7 25	8N 0				10H 1		1055		11 4			5N46		9N34		11N20	
Pebworth Halt	5 21			6 8	6 21	6 57			7 29	8N 4				10H 5				dd			5N50		9N38			
Honeybourne .. .. .. arr	5 25			6 13	6 25	7 2			7 33	8N 8				10H10		11 4		11 12			5N55		9N43		11N26	
163Evesham .... arr	5 39			6 23	6 35	7 16				8N19				10H20		1113	Saturdays only	11 23			6N 3		9N51		11N34	
163Worcester (Shrub Hill) .. „	6 11		②	7 20	7 20	7 45	②			8N50	②			10H49		1132		11 52			6N31		10N19		11N57	
Honeybourne .... dep			6 5				7 20				8 15															
Weston-sub-Edge Halt ..			6 11				nn				8 21															
Willersey Halt			6 1				nn				8 24						②									
Broadway ..			6 18		Saturdays only		7 29				8 28						1127									
Laverton Halt			6 23								8 34										Commences 1st May, 1960		Commences 1st May, 1960			
Toddington			6 28	Except Saturdays			7 37				8 39															
Hayles Abbey Halt			6 31								8 42															
Winchcombe			6 35				7 44				8 48															
Gretton Halt..........			6 39				7 48				8 52															
Bishop's Cleeve Halt			6 47				7 53				8 58															
Cheltenham Spa { Malvern Road arr		6 17	6 54				8 1				9 6		9 38						1012			7 19				
Cheltenham Spa { St. James' .. „			7 1				8 7				9 12						1155									

A Except Saturdays dep 3 33 pm
B Birmingham (Moor Street)
b Commencing 1st May, 1960, dep Leamington Spa General 5N 0 pm, Warwick 5N 4, and Hatton 5N13 pm
C On Saturdays dep 12 35 pm
dd Calls to set down only, on notice being given to the guard
H On Mondays to Fridays Second class only. On Saturdays First and Second class
N Second class only
nn Calls to set down passengers on notice being given to the Guard at Honeybourne
P On Mondays to Fridays dep 6 40 am
RC Restaurant Car
RB Buffet Car available for portion of the journey only
S Saturdays only
② Second class only

On Sundays the Birmingham and Midland Motor Omnibus Co. Ltd. operate a Road Service between Evesham and Broadway; also the Bristol Omnibus Co. Ltd. operate a Road Service between Broadway, Winchcombe and Cheltenham Spa

November 1959

HAYLES ABBEY HALT

70. The halt came into use on 24th September 1928 and is seen on 27th February 1960 along with 0-4-2T no. 1424 working the 1.17pm from Honeybourne. One of the hooks for oil lamps is visible. (E.Wilmshurst)

71. The final timetable was valid until 7th March 1960 and was photographed in Winchcombe Railway Museum. The locality is often spelt "Hailes", but not by the railway. (V.Mitchell)

72. Photographed from the same bridge is another former GWR engine. This is 0-6-0PT no. 7752 on 31st March 1991, with the 13.00 departure from Toddington. A new halt at this site was planned in 1998. (T.Heavyside)

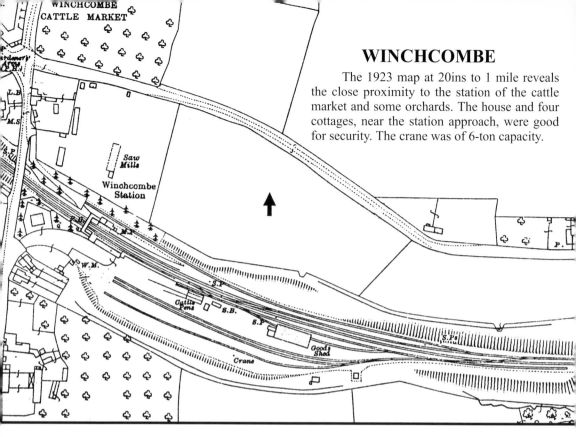

WINCHCOMBE

The 1923 map at 20ins to 1 mile reveals the close proximity to the station of the cattle market and some orchards. The house and four cottages, near the station approach, were good for security. The crane was of 6-ton capacity.

73. The starting signal at the east end of the down platform (left) would have been used ten times a day from 1st February 1905 to 1st June 1906. During this period there was a bus connection to Cheltenham. (Lens of Sutton)

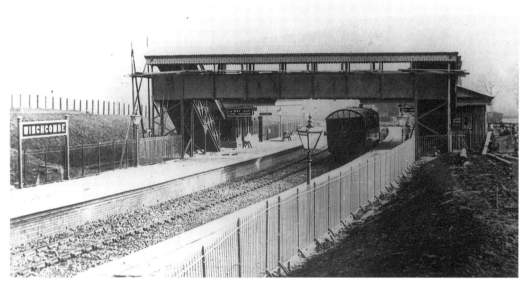

74. Another photograph from the early months shows wooden scaffolding near the footbridge and the up platform being finished. Lighting was by acetylene, the gas hut being behind the weigh house. (Lens of Sutton)

75. At last we have a close view of a steam railmotor of the type used in the early years. Their popularity was limited due to vibration from the engine and dirt from the locomotive sheds in which they were serviced. (Lens of Sutton)

76. Freight tonnage peaked at 17045 tons in 1943, unusual commodities despatched being filter paper and blotting paper. There were few passengers to be photographed in the 1950s. (J.Moss/R.Carpenter coll.)

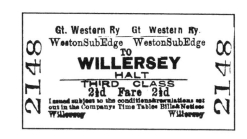

Gt. Western Ry   Gt Western Ry.
WestonSubEdge   WestonSubEdge
TO
WILLERSEY
HALT
THIRD CLASS
2½d Fare 2½d
Issued subject to the conditions&regulations set out in the Companys Time Tables Bills&Notices
Willersey   Willersey

2148   2148

77. The signal box was in use until 24th February 1965 and had 31 levers. Cattle wagons predominate in the 50-wagon up refuge siding. The coal train derailment that closed the line on 25th August 1976 took place east of the station. (J.Moss/R.C.Carpenter coll.)

78. The goods yard had closed on 2nd November 1964 but goods trains continued to pass by for another 12 years. This March 1965 picture confirms that the demolition men were quick to act, only the weigh house, dwellings and goods shed being spared. (T.David/C.L.Caddy coll.)

79. The first GWSR train had arrived on 2nd August 1987; this is the 15.00 Toddington to Gretton on 31st March 1991. Note that the signals were not yet in use and that the up platform was still being rebuilt. (T.Heavyside)

80. Three photographs from 14th August 1997 survey the station and reveal the amazing progress. Compare with picture no. 78. No. 6960 *Raveningham Hall* is bound for Gotherington and the relaid yard is full of interesting stock. (P.G.Barnes)

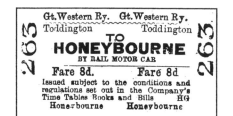

Gt. Western Ry.   Gt. Western Ry.
Toddington   Toddington

263   **TO**   263

HONEYBOURNE
BY RAIL MOTOR CAR

Fare 8d.   Fare 8d.

Issued subject to the conditions and regulations set out in the Company's Time Tables Books and Bills   HG
Honeybourne   Honeybourne

81. The building components had previously served the GWR at Monmouth Troy, the platform slabs had come from Birmingham Snow Hill and Cheltenham St. James and the signal box from Birmingham Hall Green. Its 37-lever frame was from Honeybourne West Loop Box. (P.G.Barnes)

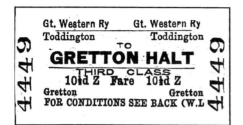

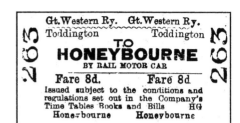

82. The bidirectional signalling was ready for commissioning. The passing loop had been operational since 12th July 1997. The trees flanking each station from Broadway southwards had been planted by the environmentally conscious GWR. (P.G.Barnes)

83. Two photographs from July 1998 show the high standard of re-creation achieved. The signalling is fully functional and a demonstration goods train is standing in the up siding. The Carriage & Wagon Dept. is on the right. (V.Mitchell)

84. The approach road was still flanked by the original weigh house and station masters house. The town centre is one mile distant, which was a factor making bus services more attractive to passengers after World War I. However, a bus link between the station, town centre and Cheltenham commenced in 1998. (V.Mitchell)

85. The Winchcombe Railway Museum is close to the church at 23 Gloucester Street and contains a multitude of exhibits from throughout Britain. A small area is illustrated, this including a Forest of Dean Railway milepost of 1826. (T.Petchey)

```
  2nd · SINGLE    SINGLE · 2nd
1          Winchcombe to           1
9   Winchcombe        Winchcombe   9
8                                  8
3   Hayles AbbeyHt   Hayles AbbeyHt 3
    HAYLES ABBEY
           HALT
    (W)  4d    Fare   4d   W)
  For conditions see over  For conditions see over
```

Winchcombe	1913	1923	1933
Passenger tickets issued	21824	15801	8367
Season tickets issued	*	206	232
Parcels forwarded	19900	21063	8656
General goods forwarded (tons)	1278	1109	486
Coal and coke received (tons)	269	514	1219
Other minerals received (tons)	2064	1565	1083
General goods received (tons)	2945	1885	1066
Trucks of livestock handled	224	141	34
(* not available)			

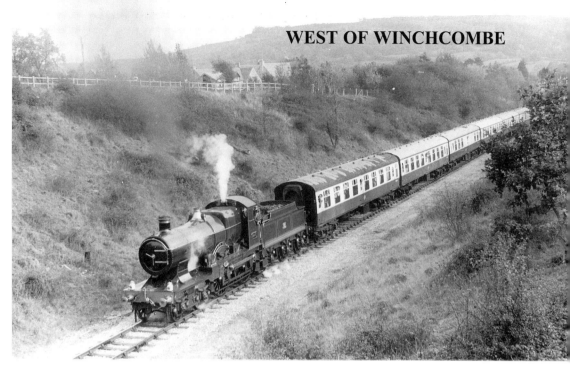

86. Our route has been at the foot of the Cotswolds, seen in the background. It turned west at Winchcombe for three miles before regaining a southerly course. First it passed through Greet Tunnel, which the visiting *City of Truro* is approaching on 13th October 1990. This is the summit of the line and is almost 300ft above sea level. (D.Trevor Rowe)

87. No. 7752 is emerging from the west portal of the 693yd long tunnel on 31st March 1991. The Blue Lias Clay was so hard that it needed blasting during the construction, but when used for embankments it proved unstable. Volunteer track layers had the unusual experience of working under cover. (T.Heavyside)

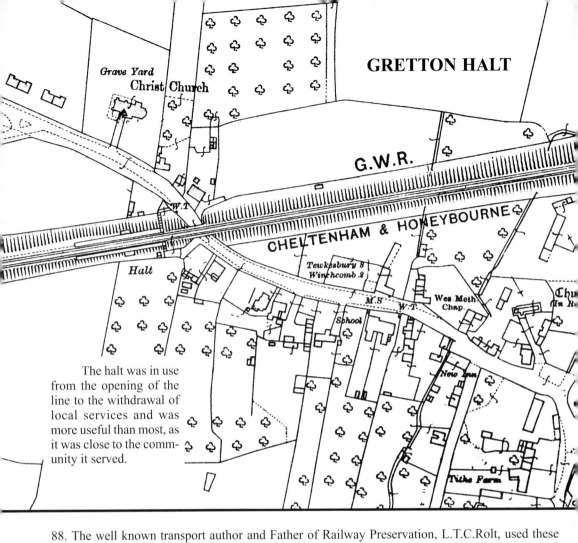

GRETTON HALT

Grave Yard
Christ Church

G.W.R.

CHELTENHAM & HONEYBOURNE

Halt

Tewkesbury 8
Winchcomb 2

M.S.   W.T.

Wes.Meth.
Chap.

School

New Inn

Tithe Farm

The halt was in use from the opening of the line to the withdrawal of local services and was more useful than most, as it was close to the community it served.

88. The well known transport author and Father of Railway Preservation, L.T.C.Rolt, used these platforms in his formative years. Tom lived at nearby Stanley Pontlarge in the late 1920s and was to influence your author (V.M.) in matters of railway appreciation and revival in the 1950s. (W.A.Camwell/M.Dart coll.)

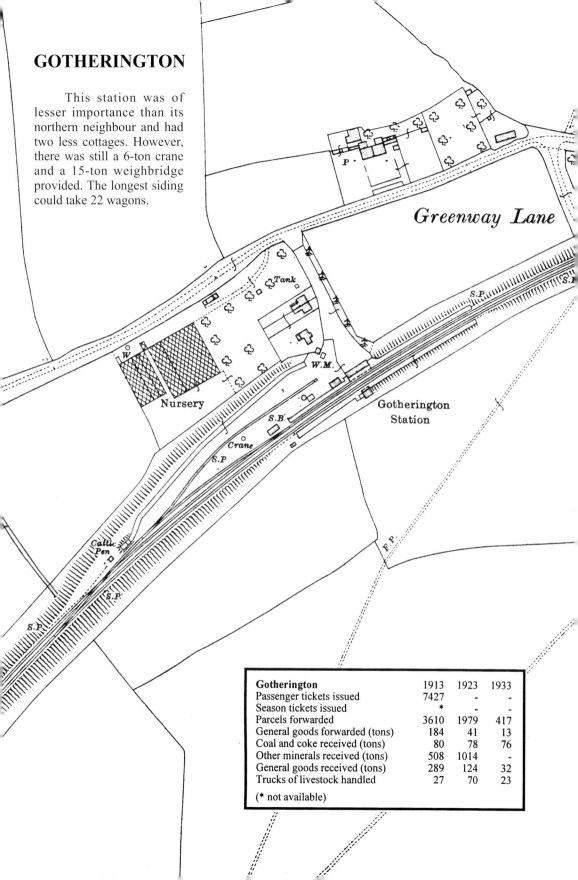

GOTHERINGTON

This station was of lesser importance than its northern neighbour and had two less cottages. However, there was still a 6-ton crane and a 15-ton weighbridge provided. The longest siding could take 22 wagons.

Greenway Lane

Gotherington
Station

Nursery

Tank

W.M.

S.B.

Crane

Cattle
Pen

Gotherington	1913	1923	1933
Passenger tickets issued	7427	-	-
Season tickets issued	*	-	-
Parcels forwarded	3610	1979	417
General goods forwarded (tons)	184	41	13
Coal and coke received (tons)	80	78	76
Other minerals received (tons)	508	1014	-
General goods received (tons)	289	124	32
Trucks of livestock handled	27	70	23
(* not available)			

89. The buildings were constructed from Cleeve Hill stone and the small goods shed was situated on the up platform. The station became unstaffed and thus a halt on 1st January 1941. (Stations UK)

Gt Western Ry.   Gt Western Ry

CHELTENHAM   CHELTENHAM
Racecourse Stn.   Racecourse Stn.

TO

BISHOPS CLEEVE

023   THIRD CLASS   023

3d. N   Fare   3d. N

Issued subject to the conditions&regulations set out in the Company's Time Tables, Bills, & Notices
Bishops Cleeve   Bishops Cleeve

91. The four photographs that follow were taken soon after trains began to run again on this section of the route on 12th July 1997. The residence had passed into the hands of a railway enthusiast, who had furnished it externally with appropriate items. (P.G.Barnes)

90. The signal box had 33 levers (20 in use) and was closed on 3rd April 1949, when the sidings were disconnected. The box had been little used for many years and the station closed completely on 13th June 1955, eventually becoming a dwelling. (Mowat coll.)

92. The booking office sign (left) was part of the collection and not an invitation to travel, as trains ran non-stop through the restored down platform to reach the loop. There was no public access here in 1998. (P.G.Barnes)

93. No. 6960 *Raveningham Hall* reverses towards the points, prior to rejoining its train. The finely restored station must make a lasting impression on the passing travellers at the end of their six-mile journey from Toddington. (P.G.Barnes)

94. Our final look at Gotherington is from the southern end of the new loop, which is likely to remain the limit of travel until the three miles to Cheltenham Race Course are completed. (M.J.Stretton)

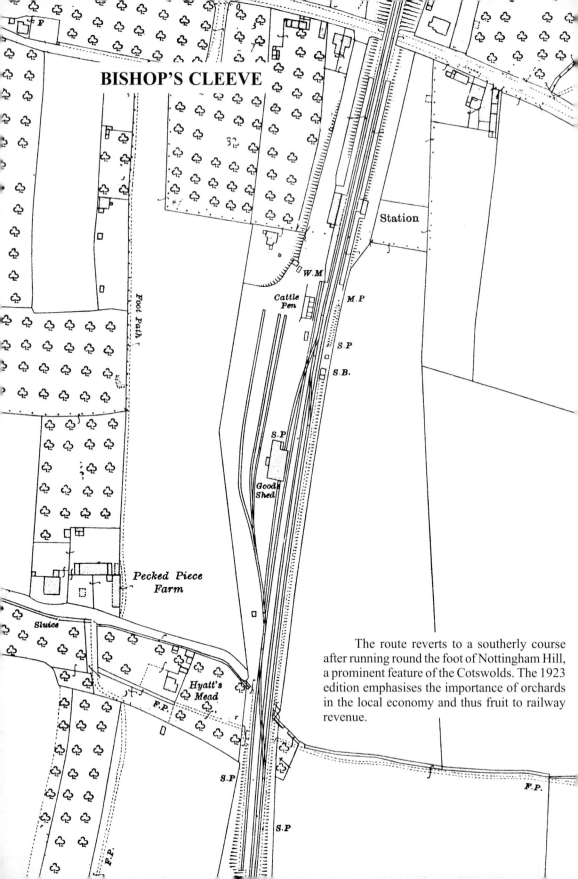

BISHOP'S CLEEVE

Station

W.M

Cattle
Pen

M.P

S.P

S.B.

S.P

Good
Shed

Foot Path

Pecked Piece
Farm

Sluice

Hyatt's
Mead

F.P.

S.P

S.P

F.P.

F.P.

The route reverts to a southerly course
after running round the foot of Nottingham Hill,
a prominent feature of the Cotswolds. The 1923
edition emphasises the importance of orchards
in the local economy and thus fruit to railway
revenue.

95. A steam railmotor stands by the down waiting shelter soon after the opening. These vehicles were capable of hauling a trailer, so most of the halts had to be extended in 1907 to accommodate the extra coach. (Lens of Sutton)

96. The fine stone came from the nearby Cleeve Hill Quarry and looked very smart when new. All stations northwards were built of brick. The station was the southern terminus from 1st June to 1st August 1906 only. Lighting was by oil and the name was etched in the glass of the lanterns. (Lens of Sutton)

97. There was no footbridge here or at Gotherington at any time but this would have not concerned the lady unloading a perambulator with the help of the guard. Staffing of the station ceased on 1st September 1950. Autotrain working ended subsequently.
(W.A.Camwell/M.Dart coll.)

Bishop's Cleeve	1913	1923	1933
Passenger tickets issued	14239	13484	11272
Season tickets issued	*	37	46
Parcels forwarded	1932	1521	2192
General goods forwarded (tons)	275	118	86
Coal and coke received (tons)	91	96	303
Other minerals received (tons)	1300	1593	790
General goods received (tons)	773	1109	1326
Trucks of livestock handled	32	39	40

(* not available)

98. A staff of five was provided in the 1930s, after the station master had been withdrawn in 1931. The station was subsequently administered from Winchcombe for many years. A local train from Cheltenham was recorded on 27th February 1960. (E.Wilmshurst)

99. Ex-LMS class 5 no. 45006 speeds north on 14th August 1965. The goods yard had closed on 1st July 1963 and the unusual stone built 31-lever signal box ceased to function on 11th August 1965. Only 22 levers had been used. The crane and weighbridge were similar to those at the stations further north. (T.David/C.L.Caddy coll.)

CHELTENHAM RACECOURSE

100. The buildings were prefabricated at the GWR's Swindon Works and the station was opened on 13th March 1912. The structures housed mostly toilets and the signal box contained just six levers, used mainly on race days until closure on 9th February 1964. Local and through trains would then make extra stops here and up to ten specials were not unknown. (Stations UK)

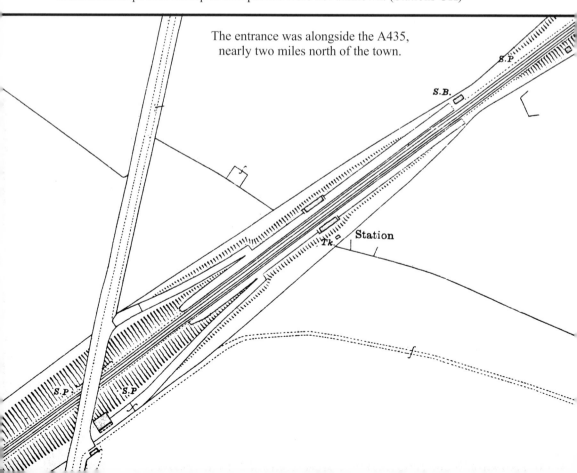

The entrance was alongside the A435, nearly two miles north of the town.

S.B.

S.P

S.P.

S.P

Tk.

Station

101. No. 6952 *Kimberley Hall* was in shabby condition when recorded working a ballast train on 19th June 1965. The station was opened regularly for race meetings until 21st March 1968 and occasionally thereafter. Horses were sometimes unloaded and loaded here but this was usually done at Bishop's Cleeve until 1935. (T.David/C.L.Caddy coll.)

102. Unlike most of the other stations, the platforms remained intact and even the booking office survived. This was photographed in 1997 after renovation. Some 100yds of track were laid to allow 0-4-2T no. 1450 to run with a van on 28th June 1998, to publicise a share issue. Hopefully this will become the southern terminus of what might become termed the InterRacecourse Railway, in due course. (P.G.Barnes)

CHELTENHAM
HIGH STREET HALT

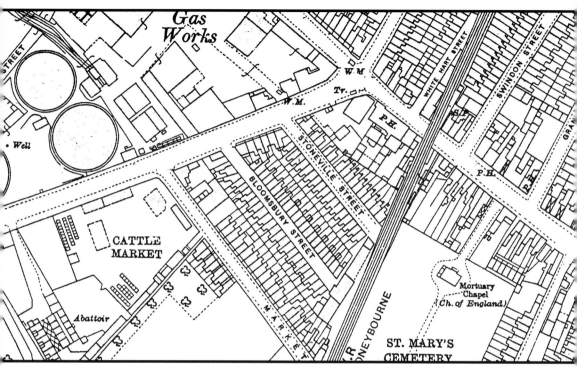

The High Street is across the right of this 1923 survey; the narrow site of the halt is to the south of the bridge over it. The 79yd long Hunting Butts Tunnel was north of the town.

103. The halt was in use from 1st October 1908 until closed by wartime conditions on 30th April 1917. This postcard view of a southbound railmotor on the bridge is the only picture known to exist. The bridge now carries a footpath. (Lens of Sutton)

CHELTENHAM SPA ST. JAMES

104. A panorama from St. George's Road bridge in 1931 includes the cattle dock, left. The two running roads are each side of the nearest signal. Broad gauge trains had ceased to run here in May 1872. Goods traffic ended on 3rd January 1966, but coal was handled until 31st October of that year. (Mowat coll.)

The 1906 route from High Street to Malvern Road crosses the top left corner of this 1923 map, which is at 20ins to 1 mile. The station was opened on 23rd October 1847 and received the suffix St. James (not St. James's Square as marked) on 11th May 1908. It was renamed Cheltenham Spa (St. James) on 1st February 1925. The goods shed contained four small cranes and the one in the yard was rated at 8 tons.

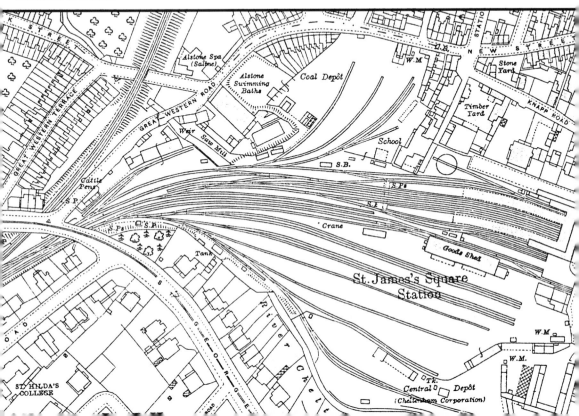

105. The elegant exterior complemented the fine architecture of the historic spa town and was decorated for the Coronation of her Majesty Queen Elizabeth II in May 1953. A Ford Popular is parked in the deserted square. (Lens of Sutton)

2nd-SINGLE SINGLE-2nd
Cheltenham Spa St. James to
CheltenhamS.St.J   CheltenhamS.St.J
Cheltenham Spa M.Rd Cheltenham Spa M.Rd
CHELTENHAM SPA. MALVERN ROAD
(W)   2d.   FARE   2d.   (W)
For conditions see over For conditions see over
3861   3861

106. The signal box is right of centre in this panoramic view and faced platform 4. Both the station and the 1920 53-lever box closed on 15th June 1966. The sign board seems to have lost its bottom rail and been refixed in a lower position. (Rail Archive Stephenson)

107. Class 5101 2-6-2T no. 4101 is reversing towards the turntable on 1st October 1960, having propelled its coaches towards the signal box. The long train at platform 2 is probably bound for London. Other through trains from this station at that time included ones to Cardiff, Kingham and Southampton in addition to local services to Gloucester. (H.C.Casserley)

108. Two photographs from 31st October 1964 include 9400 class 0-6-0PT no. 8471. Passengers having alighted at platform 3, it is about to use the crossover visible on the left. Nos 3 and 4 were the two original platforms.
(T.David/C.L.Caddy coll.)

109. Having run round on the adjacent line, the engine has returned to its train, the destination of which was not recorded. The Kingham service had been withdrawn in October 1962 and Southampton trains had ceased in September 1961, leaving Gloucester as its probable goal.
(T.David/C.L.Caddy)

110. The modern telephone kiosks and bookstall for Wymans contrasted with the detailed original tracery of the roof spans in 1965. After closure all was lost in favour of a featureless office block.
(Stations UK)

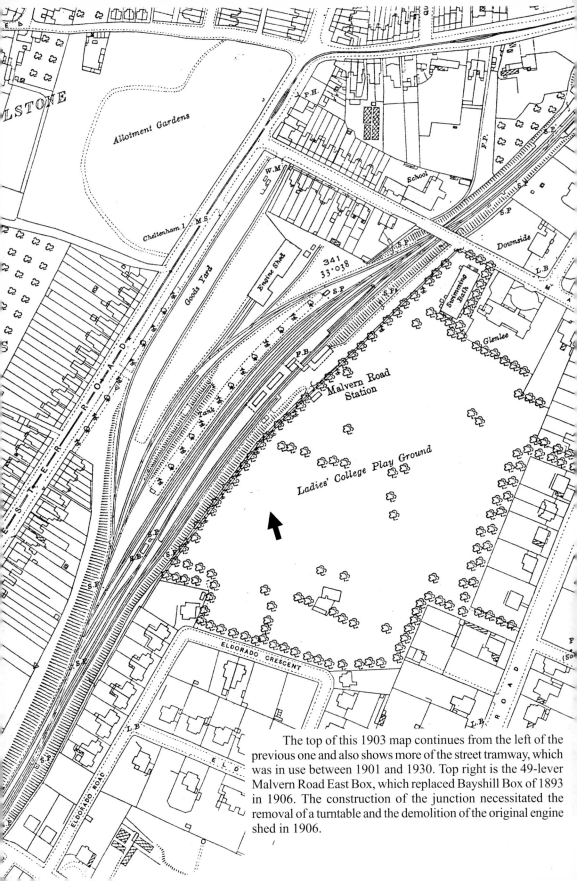

The top of this 1903 map continues from the left of the previous one and also shows more of the street tramway, which was in use between 1901 and 1930. Top right is the 49-lever Malvern Road East Box, which replaced Bayshill Box of 1893 in 1906. The construction of the junction necessitated the removal of a turntable and the demolition of the original engine shed in 1906.

CHELTENHAM SPA MALVERN ROAD

111. The station opened on 30th March 1908, more than 18 months after the route from Stratford had been completed. During that period, all trains had to reverse in or out of St. James. Subsequently only local trains did so, often reversing at this bay, seen in 1923. (Stations UK)

112. The reversing bay is seen more clearly in this panoramic view from Malvern Road bridge, taken in 1932. The engine shed is on the right. The station was closed from 1st January 1917 to 7th July 1919 as a wartime economy measure; most through trains on the route were cancelled during this period. (Mowat coll.)

113. A view in the opposite direction from the same era features the goods yard connection and the headshunt. The three sidings to the left of the platforms could each accommodate over 50 wagons. Lansdown Junction is behind the camera. (Mowat coll.)

114. The station was remote from the town centre and a Triumph Renown or an Austin 14 would have provided an ideal way to reach the premises in 1948. There was a long inclined drive down to the station. (National Railway Museum)

115. The two-road brick-built shed was opened in 1907 to succeed the one near St. James. The asbestos-clad shed was added in April 1943, when the route was carrying much additional wartime traffic. The photo was taken on 30th August 1953. (N.L.Browne)

116. Ex-GWR 2-6-2T no. 5173 can be identified in this side view of the shed roads. The shedmaster was required to provide banking engines, when necessary, for heavy goods trains climbing the incline to Bishop's Cleeve. Just as the steam railmotor's upholstery suffered from the dusty shed environment, so did the diesel railcars of a later generation. (M.Dart coll.)

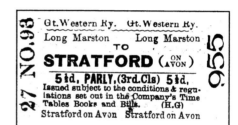

117. No. 20 was revealing her propeller shaft on 20th September 1953. The shed was closed on 2nd March 1964 and in recent years has been used by a builders merchant. (G.K.B.Green/Initial Photographs)

118. Looking north in March 1959, we can see no less than five starting signals, but there was no turntable. Small engines went to St. James and large ones used the junction triangle south of Cheltenham. The word SPA was added in 1925. (R.M.Casserley)

119. This 1960 picture was taken from the same position as the one on the cover. Note the array of distant signals. West Box was functioning from June 1908 until 3rd November 1970. It had 37 levers, a common size of frame on the route. (H.C.Casserley)

120. The station closed for goods and passengers on 3rd January 1966, but the yard was used for wagon storage and the through lines carried trains between Gloucester and Birmingham for a further two years, but the residents of Cheltenham were not allowed to use them - hence the shrub covered platform! The water column stands as a reminder of a happier age; much of the platform surface was removed by GWR Society members and is now used by steam train passengers again.
(RAS Marketing)

THE CORNISHMAN
RESTAURANT CAR SERVICE
BETWEEN
WOLVERHAMPTON, BIRMINGHAM,
GLOUCESTER, BRISTOL
AND THE
WEST OF ENGLAND
Via Stratford-upon-Avon

WEEK DAYS
MONDAYS TO FRIDAYS

	Runs until Thursday, 23rd July inclusive and from Monday, 24th August	Runs Friday, 24th July to Friday, 21st August inclusive
	am	am
WOLVERHAMPTON (Low Level) .. ..dep	9 A 0	9 A 0
Bilston Central .. .. .. ,,	9 A 6	9 A 6
Wednesbury Central.. .. .. ,,	9 A12	9 A12
West Bromwich .. .. ,,	9 A20	9 A20
Birmingham (Snow Hill) .. ,,	9 A40	9 A40
Stratford-upon-Avon .. ,,	10 19	10 19
Cheltenham Spa (Malvern Rd) ,,	11 2	11 2
Gloucester Eastgate .. .. ,,	11 20	11 20
	pm	pm
Bristol (Temple Meads) ..arr	12 15	
Taunton .. .. .. ,,	1 15	
Exeter (St. David's) .. .. ,,	1 58	B
Dawlish .. .. ,,	2 33	
Teignmouth .. .. .. ,,	2 41	
Newton Abbot .. .. .. ,,	2 51	
Torre .. .. ,,	3 11	
Torquay .. .. ,,	3 14	
Paignton .. .. .. ,,	3 24	B
Goodrington Sands Halt .. ,,	3 27	
Churston (for Brixham).. .. ,,	3 34	
Kingswear .. .. .. ,,	3 44	
Plymouth .. .. ,,	3 20	3 10
Liskeard .. .. ,,	3 59	3 49
Bodmin Road .. .. .. ,,	4 15	4 5
Par .. .. ,,	4 28	4 18
St. Austell .. .. .. ,,	4 39	4 29
Truro .. .. ,,	5 2	4 52
St. Erth .. .. ,,	5 38	5 28
Penzance .. .. ,,	5 50	5 40

	Runs until Thursday, 23rd July inclusive and from Monday, 24th August	Runs Friday, 24th July to Friday, 21st August inclusive
	am	am
PENZANCE.. .. .. ..dep	10A30	10A30
St. Erth .. .. ,,	10A40	10A40
Truro .. .. ,,	11A20	11A20
St. Austell .. .. .. ,,	11 48	11 48
Par .. .. ,,	11 57	11 57
	pm	pm
Plymouth .. .. .. ,,	1 0	1 0
Kingswear .. .. .. ,,	12A15	
Churston (for Brixham).. ,,	12A30	
Goodrington Sands Halt ,,	12 40	B
Paignton .. .. ,,	12A55	
Torquay .. .. ,,	1 A2	
Torre .. .. ,,	1 7	
Kingskerswell .. .. .. ,,	1 15	
Newton Abbot .. .. .. ,,	1 23	
Teignmouth .. .. .. ,,	1 34	
Dawlish.. .. .. .. ,,	1 42	B
Exeter (St. David's) .. .. ,,	2 24	
Taunton .. .. ,,	3 5	
Bristol (Temple Meads) .. ,,	4 8	
Gloucester Eastgate .. ..arr	5 3	3 52
Cheltenham Spa (Malvern Rd) ,,	5 21	4 40
Stratford-upon-Avon .. ,,	6 5	5 0
Birmingham (Snow Hill) .. ,,	6 49	5 50
West Bromwich .. .. ,,	7 4	6 33
Wednesbury Central.. .. ,,	7 12	..
Bilston Central .. .. .. ,,	7 18	..
Wolverhampton (Low Level) ,,	7 25	7 3

A—Seats can be reserved in advance on payment of a fee of 2s. 0d. per seat

B—See Table 169 for service on these dates.

Easebourne Lane, Midhurst, West Sussex. GU29 9AZ Tel: 01730 813169 Fax: 01730 812601
If books are not available from your local transport stockist, order direct with cheque, Visa or Mastercard, post free UK.

BRANCH LINES
Branch Line to Allhallows
Branch Lines to Alton
Branch Lines around Ascot
Branch Line to Ashburton
Branch Lines around Bodmin
Branch Line to Bude
Branch Lines around Canterbury
Branch Line to Cheddar
Branch Lines to East Grinstead
Branch Lines to Effingham Junction
Branch Line to Fairford
Branch Line to Hawkhurst
Branch Line to Hayling
Branch Lines to Horsham
Branch Line to Ilfracombe
Branch Line to Kingswear
Branch Lines to Launceston & Princetown
Branch Lines to Longmoor
Branch Lines to Looe
Branch Line to Lyme Regis
Branch Lines around Midhurst
Branch Line to Minehead
Branch Lines to Newport (IOW)
Branch Line to Padstow
Branch Lines around Plymouth
Branch Lines to Seaton & Sidmouth
Branch Line to Selsey
Branch Lines around Sheerness
Branch Line to Tenterden
Branch Lines to Torrington
Branch Lines to Tunbridge Wells
Branch Line to Upwell
Branch Lines around Weymouth
Branch Lines around Wimborne
Branch Lines around Wisbech

NARROW GAUGE BRANCH LINES
Branch Line to Lynton
Branch Lines around Portmadoc 1923-46
Branch Lines around Porthmadog 1954-94
Branch Line to Southwold
Two-Foot Gauge Survivors

SOUTH COAST RAILWAYS
Ashford to Dover
Brighton to Eastbourne
Chichester to Portsmouth
Dover to Ramsgate
Hastings to Ashford
Portsmouth to Southampton
Ryde to Ventnor
Worthing to Chichester

SOUTHERN MAIN LINES
Bromley South to Rochester
Charing Cross to Orpington
Crawley to Littlehampton
Dartford to Sittingbourne
East Croydon to Three Bridges
Epsom to Horsham
Exeter to Barnstaple
Exeter to Tavistock
Faversham to Dover
Haywards Heath to Seaford
London Bridge to East Croydon
Orpington to Tonbridge
Swanley to Ashford
Tavistock to Plymouth
Victoria to East Croydon
Waterloo to Windsor

Waterloo to Woking
Woking to Portsmouth
Woking to Southampton
Yeovil to Exeter

EASTERN MAIN LINES
Fenchurch Street to Barking

COUNTRY RAILWAY ROUTES
Andover to Southampton
Bournemouth to Evercreech Jn.
Burnham to Evercreech Junction
Croydon to East Grinstead
Didcot to Winchester
Fareham to Salisbury
Frome to Bristol
Guildford to Redhill
Porthmadog to Blaenau
Reading to Basingstoke
Reading to Guildford
Redhill to Ashford
Salisbury to Westbury
Stratford Upon Avon to Cheltenham
Strood to Paddock Wood
Taunton to Barnstaple
Wenford Bridge to Fowey
Westbury to Bath
Woking to Alton
Yeovil to Dorchester

GREAT RAILWAY ERAS
Ashford from Steam to Eurostar
Clapham Junction 50 years of change
Festiniog in the Fifties
Festiniog in the Sixties
Isle of Wight Lines 50 years of change
Railways to Victory 1944-46

LONDON SUBURBAN RAILWAYS
Caterham and Tattenham Corner
Charing Cross to Dartford
Clapham Jn. to Beckenham Jn.
Crystal Palace and Catford Loop
East London Line
Finsbury Park to Alexandra Palace
Holborn Viaduct to Lewisham
Kingston and Hounslow Loops
Lewisham to Dartford
Lines around Wimbledon
London Bridge to Addiscombe
North London Line
South London Line
West Croydon to Epsom
West London Line
Willesden Junction to Richmond
Wimbledon to Epsom

STEAM PHOTOGRAPHERS
O.J.Morris's Southern Railways 1919-59

STEAMING THROUGH
Steaming through Cornwall
Steaming through East Sussex
Steaming through the Isle of Wight
Steaming through Kent
Steaming through West Hants
Steaming through West Sussex

TRAMWAY CLASSICS
Aldgate & Stepney Tramways
Barnet & Finchley Tramways
Bath Tramways

Bournemouth & Poole Tramways
Brighton's Tramways
Bristol's Tramways
Camberwell & W.Norwood Tramway
Clapham & Streatham Tramways
Dover's Tramways
East Ham & West Ham Tramways
Edgware and Willesden Tramways
Eltham & Woolwich Tramways
Embankment & Waterloo Tramways
Enfield & Wood Green Tramways
Exeter & Taunton Tramways
Gosport & Horndean Tramways
Greenwich & Dartford Tramways
Hampstead & Highgate Tramways
Hastings Tramways
Holborn & Finsbury Tramways
Ilford & Barking Tramways
Kingston & Wimbledon Tramways
Lewisham & Catford Tramways
Liverpool Tramways 1. Eastern Routes
Liverpool Tramways 2. Southern Routes
Maidstone & Chatham Tramways
North Kent Tramways
Portsmouth's Tramways
Reading Tramways
Seaton & Eastbourne Tramways
Southampton Tramways
Southend-on-sea Tramways
Southwark & Deptford Tramways
Stamford Hill Tramways
Thanet's Tramways
Victoria & Lambeth Tramways
Waltham Cross & Edmonton Tramwa
Walthamstow & Leyton Tramways
Wandsworth & Battersea Tramways

TROLLEYBUS CLASSICS
Croydon Trolleybuses
Bournemouth Trolleybuses
Maidstone Trolleybuses
Reading Trolleybuses
Woolwich & Dartford Trolleybuses

WATERWAY ALBUMS
Kent and East Sussex Waterways
London's Lost Route to the Sea
London to Portsmouth Waterway
Surrey Waterways
West Sussex Waterways

MILITARY BOOKS
Battle over Portsmouth
Battle over Sussex 1940
Blitz over Sussex 1941-42
Bombers over Sussex 1943-45
Bognor at War
Military Defence of West Sussex
Secret Sussex Resistance
Sussex Home Guard

OTHER BOOKS
Betwixt Petersfield & Midhurst
Brickmaking in Sussex
Changing Midhurst
Garraway Father & Son
Index to all Stations
South Eastern & Chatham Railways
London Chatham & Dover Railway

SOUTHERN RAILWAY VIDE
War on the Line